NEW ZEALAND'S
NORTH & SOUTH ISLANDS

CRAIG POTTON PUBLISHING

This booklet has no greater ambitions than to take its readers on a brief journey around the North and South Islands of New Zealand. It is intended first and foremost as a pictorial souvenir containing what we hope are the kind of images that visitors would like to carry away with them when they leave, and those who live here would be happy to send to distant friends. This booklet has been produced by joining two previously published titles on both islands into a single publication.

Published by Craig Potton Publishing,
P.O. Box 555, Nelson.

All photography by Craig Potton except:
Andy Dennis: p.47 (top), p.57 (bottom) p.62 (bottom left),
p.66 (top and above), p.69 (top).
Shantytown: p.47 (bottom)
Andrew Conway: p.52 (bottom left).
Alpine Recreation Canterbury: p.62 (top).
Michael de Hamel: p.65 (bottom right).

Text: Andy Dennis and Annie Wheeler.
Production: Andy Dennis, Robbie Burton, David Chowdhury.

Typeset by Progressive Printing.
Printed by Printgroup Wellington Ltd.

ISBN 0-908802-17-10

NEW ZEALAND'S NORTH ISLAND

The North Island is the most intensively settled and developed of New Zealand's two main islands. Its population is nearly three times that of the South Island. Its milder climate, extensive areas of low-lying land, and many sheltered harbours, bays and estuaries attracted the first Polynesian settlers over a thousand years ago, and later immigrants from Europe. Those early visitors would have been greeted by a pristine coastline and lands covered with dense native forests. Today's visitors meet a more modified landscape, but one still rich in natural wonders and where large pockets of wilderness lie close to the edges of towns and cities. The images in this booklet will give a taste for, and nurture memories of, the extraordinary diversity of the North Island landscape and its people – its giant kauri trees and spectacular beaches of the north, the mountainous volcanoes, hot pools and geysers of the Central North Island, its remote and splendid wilderness areas, and its multicultural communities.

INSIDE FRONT COVER: Cape Reinga, at the northern tip of New Zealand, is the "place of leaping", the final departing point for spirits of the Maori dead as they return to their ancestral homeland.

BELOW: This peaceful rural scene, typical of large parts of the North Island country-side, is dominated by Mt Ruapehu. At 2797m, this volcanic cone is the North Island's highest mountain.

TOP: Pacific Ocean swells stretch as if forever along the golden sands of Ninety Mile Beach, in reality closer to 90km in length.

LEFT: Polynesian peoples were the first to settle New Zealand. They developed carving as a high art form, often depicting ancestral figures.

RIGHT: Tane Mahuta "God of the Forest", rises 51m high with a girth of 14m, and is believed to be over 1200 years old. Such giant kauri trees covered the northern region of the North Island before Europeans arrived and felled them for their superb timber.

The long, narrow and indented peninsula of Northland is dominated by the coast, with nowhere further than a few kilometres from the sea. Sheltered bays and islands on the east coast, such as Motuarohia Island in the Bay of Islands (TOP LEFT) contrasts with the wild grandeur of the west coast (BOTTOM LEFT), where the sun sets over the Tasman Sea at Hokianga Harbour's South Head.

Northland was a centre of Maori population when the first European missionaries arrived, and small weatherboard churches soon sprang up across the countryside. ABOVE: This church near Pakanae is still in use, as is the St James Church behind the historic Kerikeri Stone Store (TOP RIGHT). The stone house is one of Northland's earliest colonial buildings – completed in the mid 1830s. Today, Northland is sparsely populated with small scattered rural communities where horses are a common means of farm transport (BOTTOM RIGHT).

Auckland is New Zealand's largest city, and home for nearly a third of its population. The modern high-rise city centre (TOP LEFT) is built around the edges of the Waitemata Harbour, spanned by the 1030m Auckland Harbour Bridge (BOTTOM LEFT). The city is sited on an old volcanic field from which more than 50 volcanoes have erupted. Auckland's youngest volcano, Rangitoto Island (ABOVE), erupted from the sea as recently as 600 years ago.

Maori and Polynesian peoples comprise over 10 percent of Auckland's population. TOP RIGHT: Maori men carrying paddles prepare to launch a waka (traditional canoe) at a ceremony on the Auckland waterfront. A recent wave of migration to New Zealand has brought new settlers from Pacific Islands like Fiji, Tonga, Niue and the Cook Islands. Faces at the Otara Market (BOTTOM RIGHT) reflect the city's multiculturalism.

European traditions are evident in the Mission Bay fountain on the Auckland waterfront (TOP), *and the Auckland War Memorial Museum (ABOVE).*

Sheltered waters close to Auckland offer some of the best coastal sailing in the world. The "City of Sails" hosts many international and local sailing races, including the Whitbread Round-the-World race (TOP). One in every ten Aucklanders owns a boat, and most of the more expensive craft are berthed at the city's Westhaven Marina (BOTTOM).

Ancient volcanic landforms in the Coromandel hinterland have weathered to create dramatic forms like this forest volcanic "plug" (ABOVE LEFT). The Coromandel Penisula, with its bush covered hills and many beautiful sandy beaches like those near Pauanui (BELOW LEFT), is a popular place to"get away from it all". Nearby in the Bay of Plenty, Mount Maunganui (ABOVE) near Tauranga, is New Zealand's largest export port. The rich soils and mild climate of the Bay of Plenty have made this region a centre of kiwifruit cultivation (RIGHT). Just offshore, White Island, the most active volcano in New Zealand, steams continuously (BELOW RIGHT), and periodically explodes in more significant eruptions.

Nostalgic European immigrants succeeded in making parts of the Waikato look like the English countryside. ABOVE: A stately riverboat on the Waikato River, New Zealand's longest river at 425km. LEFT: Introduced macrocarpa trees form a gracious avenue to a homestead in Cambridge, and (TOP RIGHT) an oak shelters cattle on a Waikato farm. Waikato is a major centre for dairy farming in New Zealand. BOTTOM RIGHT: Sun sets on the peaceful waters of Lake Karapiro, one of several artificial lakes on the Waikato River created for hydro-electricity generation.

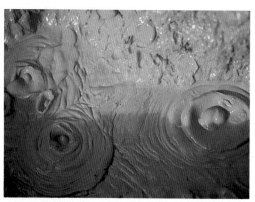

The Rotorua district is a geothermal centre, where subterranean forces break through to the earth's surface as sulphurous steam, boiling mud, hot pools, mud volcanoes and geysers. ABOVE: Champagne Pool at Waiotapu; TOP LEFT: boiling mud; and RIGHT: one of the many geysers which have made Rotorua famous worldwide, turning the district into a bubbling tourist destination.

The region is also a centre for Maori traditional arts and culture. BOTTOM LEFT: This Maori carving is in a naturalistic style, showing European influences.

The North Island displays many natural wonders. ABOVE: Limestone country around Waitomo has eroded over centuries to create a remarkable system of caves, whose stalactites and underground caverns attract thousands of visitors each year. LEFT: Attached to single strands of rope, two cavers make the spectacular descent into the entrance of Waitomo's "Lost World" cave system. TOP RIGHT: New Zealand's tallest and densest stands of lowland podocarp forests are found at Whirinaki. Such forests once flourished across North Island lowlands, but are now reduced to a few remnants.

BOTTOM RIGHT: The mighty Waikato River narrows to a mere 15m and plunges over the spectacular Huka Falls in the Wairakei Tourist park near Taupo.

Spring-flowering kowhai graces the edge of Lake Taupo in the Central North Island. New Zealand's largest lake is a gigantic crater that was the site of one of the world's largest volcanic eruptions (ABOVE). The lake and its tributary rivers are popular for trout fishing, while (LEFT) other visitors explore the lake. On the western shore (BOTTOM) a river-boat nears dramatic volcanic cliffs into which a rock carving, a contemporary interpretation of Maori mythology, has been etched. TOP RIGHT: Much of the area surrounding Taupo is sheep farming country. BOTTOM RIGHT: A Ratana church – built by followers of a Maori healer and charismatic in the early 1900s.

A chain of volcanoes in the Central North Island creates a zone of fire – the southernmost reach of the "Pacific Ring of Fire". TOP: The classically-shaped cone of Ngauruhoe catches the early morning light, with Mt Ruapehu in the background, and (TOP RIGHT) looking along the "line of fire" from the opposite direction, with Ruapehu, the highest peak, in the foreground.

ABOVE LEFT: Steam rises from the boiling waters of Mt Ngauruhoe's crater lake, leaving no doubt that this is still an active volcano. Visitors flock to Tongariro National Park, either to ski at one of Mt Ruapehu's three ski areas (ABOVE RIGHT), or to enjoy one of the park's many walks (BOTTOM RIGHT).

Tongariro National Park was New Zealand's first national park. It was created in 1887 to protect much of the Central North Island mountain landscape. ABOVE: The perfect andesitic cone of Mt Ngauruhoe rises beyond Blue Lake and Red Crater, with the snow-streaked slopes of Mt Ruapehu in the background. BELOW: A waterfall plunges down a steep rock face on Mt Ruapehu. RIGHT: An ancient beech spreads its canopy – beech is the main tree in the park.

TOP LEFT: *Evening light colours the flanks of Mt Taranaki, a dormant volcanic cone that dominates the surrounding region and its city, New Plymouth (ABOVE). The Taranaki countryside is some of the richest dairy land in New Zealand (BOTTOM RIGHT). The 198m New Plymouth power station chimney (RIGHT) dominates the city's skyline, even dwarfing the nearby Paritutu rock. Exploratory rigs like the one seen offshore are a common sight in the wake of oil and gas discoveries which have been a recent source of wealth for the region. (RIGHT). The Marokopa Falls cascade over a limestone bluff in forest near Waitomo in the King Country (BOTTOM LEFT).*

LEFT: Relentless swells of the Tasman Sea pound the western coastline north of New Plymouth. TOP: The Whanganui River begins its 290km journey on the flanks of Mt Tongariro and cuts through steep limestone gorges and picturesque river flats until it reaches the West Coast. Jetboating is a popular way to explore the river (ABOVE LEFT). The "Bridge to No-where" (ABOVE RIGHT) was built by early European settlers and is now used by trampers exploring the Whanganui National Park.

The Te Urewera National Park protects the largest remaining native forest wilderness in the North Island. At the heart of the 205,000ha park are several beautiful lakes including the island studded Lake Waikareiti (RIGHT), and the larger Lake Waikaremoana. On the park's edge, Whirinaki forest's rich soils and high rainfall support a luxuriant understorey of ferns (ABOVE). LEFT: Kahikatea trees thrive on the watery margins of the Kaitoke swamp in Whirinaki forest.

TOP: *Wind and water sculpt the soft rock of Marau Point, near Tokomaru Bay, East Cape.*

ABOVE: *A carved Maori food house guards an ancient and sacred pohutukawa tree.*

TOP: Cape Kidnappers, famous for its gannet colony, marks the southern end of Hawkes Bay.

ABOVE: Napier, Hawkes Bay's main city, is famous for its fine art deco architecture.

Wairarapa's eastern coast in the southeast of the North Island is wild and remote. Calm seas on the coast at Castlepoint (ABOVE) belie the fact that this is one of New Zealand's most treacherous boating coastlines. Early morning mist rises above fields north of Waipawa (LEFT) while a brooding sky gathers intensity over farmland north of Bulls (TOP RIGHT). Once-prosperous farming settlements throughout the North Island are increasingly abandoned, and colonial buildings like the Mangaweka general store near Taihape have lost their former glory (BOTTOM RIGHT).

Wellington is New Zealand's capital city and commercial centre. The city centre and Port Nicholson are seen from the heights of Mt Victoria (TOP LEFT), while pleasure boats moor in sheltered waters along Oriental Parade (BOTTOM LEFT). Old and new architectural styles create dramatic contrasts – restored wooden houses from the Victorian era climb the sides of steep hills overlooking Oriental Bay (TOP), while the "Beehive", the seat of New Zealand's Government (ABOVE), and the high rise BNZ tower (RIGHT), present modern, glassy styles.

ABOVE: The cabbage tree and flax, symbols of the New Zealand coast, pictured at Paipatonga. BELOW: Prevailing southwesterlies drive a cap of cloud onto the hills of Wellington's southwest coast – these winds are also responsible for the city's "windy" reputation.

THE NORTH ISLAND
Te Ika a Maui (The Fish of Maui)

TOTAL AREA: 115,777sq km
POPULATION: 2,553,413
HIGHEST MOUNTAIN: Mt Ruapehu 2797m
LONGEST RIVER: Waikato 425 km
LARGEST LAKE: Taupo 606 sq km
NATIONAL AND MARITIME PARKS: Bay of
Islands Maritime and Historic Park, Hauraki Gulf
Maritime Park, Tongariro National Park, Whanganui
National Park, Egmont National Park,
Te Urewera National Park

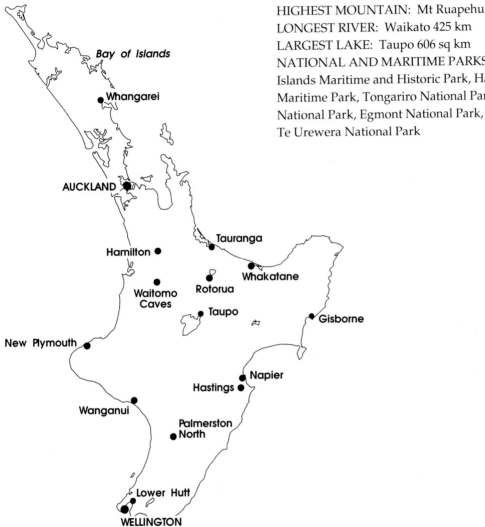

CLIMATE:

	RAINFALL	SUNSHINE	TEMP	
			(Max and Min)	
Auckland	1185mm	2070hrs	23.7	7.8
Napier	815mm	2245hrs	23.9	4.6
New Plymouth	2165mm	2165hrs	21.5	5.4
Wellington	1230mm	2040hrs	20.1	5.6

AVERAGE YEARLY FIGURES (SOURCE – 92 YEARBOOK)

NEW ZEALAND'S SOUTH ISLAND

Our main objective has been to try and convey something of the essence of the wild landscapes of the South Island, its coastline, mountains, rivers, lakes, forests, fiords and glaciers. It has now been repeated so often by visitors to have become almost axiomatic that New Zealand contains a greater diversity of unspoilt natural landscapes than any other country of comparable size, a reputation that rests to a large extent on the contribution of the South Island. It is for this reason that we have chosen to begin our journey on the West Coast seascape at the foot of this page, and the glaciated mountain scene to the left, we think there is much not only of the essence but indeed the quintessence of the South Island, bearing in mind that even some of the more striking land-scapes of the east were fashioned by glacial ice (like the Mount Cook region and the Canterbury Plains) while others which are now covered with tawny tussocks were once as green with forest as the country behind Bruce Bay.*

(*To the Maori the South Island was Te Wai Pounamu, "The waters of Greenstone", a reference to West Coast rivers that contained boulders of the highly prized greenstone. Thus for the Maori too the essence of the South Island was to be found west of the Southern Alps.)

LEFT: Evening shadows steal across the ice-fields at the head of the Fox Glacier dominated by Mt Tasman. BELOW: The serene solitude of South Westland – the beach at Bruce Bay on a winter afternoon. FOLLOWING PAGES: Westland National Park's Lake Matheson mirrors the summits of the two highest mountains in New Zealand, Mt Cook (3764m) and, to its left, Mt Tasman (3498m).

Much of the West Coast has been little modified by human intrusion and the overwhelming impression is of a region where, by and large, nature continues to rule. ABOVE: The glorious sweep of wilderness beach, wetland and lowland forest at Ohinemaka in South Westland. TOP: The curious Pancake Rocks at Punakaiki on the scenic coastline between Greymouth and Westport. RIGHT: Rainforest interior near Haast.

A remarkable feature of the West Coast is the intrusion of major glaciers down into the realms of temperate rainforest terminating a mere 300m above sea level. For over a century the Franz Josef (RIGHT) and Fox glaciers have been a major New Zealand tourist attraction (LEFT). Moreover, like Lake Moeraki (TOP), much of the lowland landscape of this part of the country is a direct legacy of the advance and retreat of very much larger ice age glaciers which at their peak flowed out from most major valleys in South Westland to beyond the present coastline.

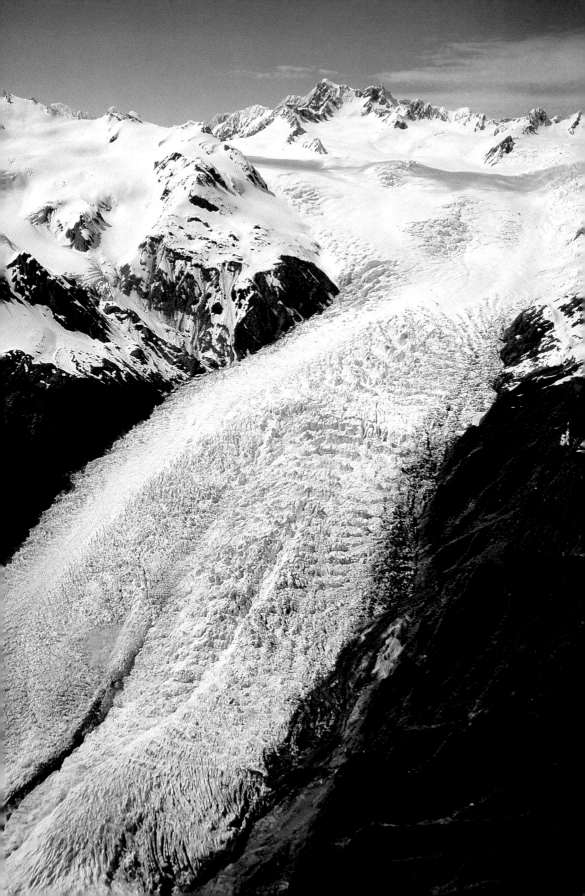

As West Coasters seek to balance a history of extraction of natural resources (greenstone, gold, coal, native timbers) with an increased emphasis on tourism, the range of tourist attractions is expanding, particularly at the northern end of "The Coast". The beautiful limestone lowlands of the recent Paparoa National Park (LEFT) and an exciting range of new outdoor adventures — like rafting the Karamea River (TOP) — help to extend the length of tourist visits to this region. So too do folk museums and other reconstructions of the West Coast's colourful past, like Coaltown in Westport or Shantytown near Greymouth (ABOVE).

ABOVE: Autumn reflections in Lake Hawea on the Haast Pass road. RIGHT: Sunset on Mt Aspiring (3027m), a glorious peak at the head of Lake Wanaka sometimes called the "Matterhorn of New Zealand".

The european settlement of both the West Coast and Central Otago was triggered by gold rushes, an era recalled by old miners' cottages in Arrowtown (TOP). But in physical terms the two regions present striking contrasts. In place of the continuous forest mantle of the West Coast, Central Otago is dominated by dry tussock landscapes, like those on the barren Pisa Range south of Wanaka (LEFT) or the legendary Skippers road near Queenstown (ABOVE).

In both summer and winter Queenstown is the South Island's leading tourist town, famed for both its dramatic setting and for the range of adventures for which it provides a base. TOP: The classic panorama of Queenstown, Lake Wakatipu and The Remarkables mountains from the Skyline Restaurant. RIGHT: Striking autumn colours on the shores of Lake Hayes. ABOVE: Jet-boating in the Shotover Canyon. LEFT: The Treble Cone skifield above Lake Wanaka.

A vast wilderness of glaciated mountains, fiords, forests, lakes and tumbling streams, the 1.2 million hectares of Fiordland National Park is considerably larger than the other seven South Island national parks added together. LEFT: A rain-swollen waterfall plunges down the precipitous walls of Milford Sound. TOP: Milford Sound overshadowed by Mitre Peak to the left and Mt Pembroke, snow-capped to the right. RIGHT: The Milford Track wends its way through the beech forests of the Clinton Valley.

The detail and grandeur of the Fiordland landscape: Mackay Falls on the Milford Track (TOP), typical of the countless streams and torrents that tumble down the flanks of the Fiordland mountains. ABOVE: The brooding majesty of Lake Manapouri and the Kepler Mountains.

TOP: The granite tor of Magog in the remote wilderness of southern Stewart Island. ABOVE: Nugget Point on Southland's wild Catlins coast, a beautiful region of forests, beaches and bold sea cliffs, less modified by settlement than any other part of the South Island's eastern coastline.

Neither the grandiose Larnach Castle on Otago Peninsula (MIDDLE RIGHT) nor the terraced houses in central Dunedin (BOTTOM RIGHT) could be described as "typical New Zealand architecture". They reflect rather a lingering nostalgia among Otago's Scottish settlers for the land they had left behind. The rapid spread of sheep across the New Zealand landscape (TOP LEFT) must also have made them feel more at home as would parts of the Otago coastline, like the outer coast of Otago Peninsula (BOTTOM LEFT) or Moeraki to the north (TOP RIGHT), the latter famous for the curious large spherical boulders lying half buried in its sands.

ABOVE: Ranges and valleys of tawny windswept tussock line the Lindis Pass, southern gateway to the Mount Cook region. TOP: The summit ridge of Aoraki (or Mt Cook) on a winter evening. LEFT: An old beech tree in winter garb near Mount Cook village.

TOP: Trampers climb above the Tasman Glacier on a guided crossing of Ball Pass. LEFT: The Beetham Hut and the rocky ramparts of Malte Brun (3156m) in a tributary valley of the Tasman Glacier. RIGHT: Morning light on the ice-plastered eastern faces of Mt Tasman (3498m). ABOVE: A landscape worn smooth by vanished ice-age glaciers – the Two Thumb Range on the eastern side of Lake Tekapo.

The lunchtime antics of Christchurch's official wizard in Cathedral Square (TOP) and the stately homestead and grounds of Mona Vale (ABOVE) suggest a balance of eccentricity and tradition which constitutes much of the charm of the South Island's largest population centre. Southeast of the city lies Banks Peninsula whose rolling hills and deep harbours (like Akaroa Harbour RIGHT) are the eroded remnants of long-extinct volcanoes. Before the last ice ages Banks Peninsula was an island, eventually linked to the Southern Alps by the spread of glacial outwash gravels that now make up the pastoral patchwork of the Canterbury Plains (LEFT).

TOP LEFT: The kea, delinquent comedian of the South Island mountains. ABOVE: the giant mountain buttercup flowers on the summit of Arthur's Pass from November to January. LEFT: The Devil's Punchbowl Falls near Arthur's Pass village. TOP RIGHT: The Ada Valley near the Lewis Pass, a typical eastern Southern Alps landscape of open river flats, uniform beech forest and rapidly eroding greywacke ranges with widespread screes. BOTTOM RIGHT: Lake Sumner near dusk with a northwest storm brewing.

TOP LEFT: Kaikoura is the only place in the world where sperm whales can be seen close inshore throughout the year. Further north in the Marlborough Sounds (TOP RIGHT and BOTTOM RIGHT), sanctuary islands protect several endangered plants and animals including the tuatara (ABOVE), a unique survivor from the age of the dinosaurs. BOTTOM LEFT: the Wairau River near Blenheim flows in a shifting pattern of braided channels, typical of many eastern South Island rivers.

Nelson has two national parks, two very large forest parks and a maritime park all less than two hours' drive away. TOP: The peace of an autumn morning at Lake Rotoiti in Nelson Lakes National Park. ABOVE: Wave-patterned tidal sandbanks at the entrance to Awaroa Inlet, Abel Tasman National Park. RIGHT: The crescent beaches of Anchorage and Te Pukatea bays, also from Abel Tasman National Park.

Scenes from Nelson and Golden Bay — TOP: A fishing boat departs at dusk from Port Nelson, New Zealand's foremost fishing port. MIDDLE LEFT: The Chez Eelco coffee house, a congenial part of Nelson's culinary and cultural landscape. BOTTOM LEFT: Dairy pasture and kiwi fruit orchards on the banks of the Takaka River in Golden Bay. TOP RIGHT: An old derelict homestead at the edge of the Waimea Plain. BOTTOM RIGHT: Cattle and windshorn pines on a farm near Paturau in the western part of Golden Bay.

TOP: Luxurious coastal forest bordering the Big River estuary on the western coast of Golden Bay. ABOVE: Farewell Spit, the 25-kilometre sandspit at the norwestern extremity of the South Island, which is protected as a Wetland of International Importance for migratory wading birds.